The Grass that Grows in Sidewalks

M W

BookLeaf Publishing

Presentation by *BookLeaf Publishing*

Web: www.bookleafpub.com

E-mail: info@bookleafpub.com

ISBN: 9789357210881

First edition 2022

I dedicate this to all of the people I've walked by in life— every single one of you has influenced me in some sort of way.

ACKNOWLEDGEMENT

Thank you to my brother for being my biggest supporter and being there for me as we've gotten through life side by side ever since I can remember.

Thanks to my best friends, Jenna, Joel, and Dillion for always being an eager audience and helping me out through the hardest parts of life I have lived during my 20s.

Thank you to Ashly for showing me this writing contest-- this is finally going to get me going on my chapbook!

Thank you to Lincoln, Kaitlyn, Nick, Liz, and Ryan for assisting with some of my poems' names, and any other friends whom I've also shown my poetry to, especially Mitch, Nick, Jon, Mason, and anyone else who ever cared to read.

Thank you to all my professors I had in college (Tim, Ryan, Melanie, Rebecca, Leanne specifically) who helped me curate my writing when I was in school. Also thank you to every fellow student I worked with in classes, from praise, suggestions, and critiques-- any minute was never wasted.

Thank you to all my classmates and members of the WWC (Warriors Writing Club): Myriah, Ellie, Rakaila, Keisha, Gary, Kaitlyn, Sam, Willie, Jeremy, Donnica, Ruth, Diana, Jacobi, Madina, Hattie, Sabrina, Rae, and to anyone else whose name I'm unfortunately forgetting.

Thank you to Jake for helping support my household and accepting my struggles along with your own. Nowhere to build but upright now. Even if you don't like poetry, you've stuck by all my struggles and hardships in life and hugged me at 4:30 AM when I selected all my poems for this book. You're the wild card for the inspiration of my angst and I will always love you for that no matter what.

Thank you to my favorite band, Modest Mouse, for inspiring me to strive for a purpose to reflect my own emotions and experiences in writing; thank you for filling the silence with something that extracts every ounce of the human existence into music. This goes to all the other bands I love too.

Thank you to my son, Elijah. Possibly the biggest support to make sure I get up and eat every morning. Thank you for helping me see life through a child's lens.

Thank you to my Mom who gave me this current life. May she rest in peace while I keep the fire going.

PREFACE

When I think of any themes I've noticed in my poetry, the first ones to pop up are always toward smoking, nature, street lamps and other human-made necessities, walking, and in the last few years, driving to manifest my emotions in a way where I can just beat around the bush as an effortless attempt to vocalize how I feel. Going beyond those symbolic favorites, I think I tend to really hide to mention my struggle for pure thoughts between myself, life, and death. Emotions always come to play but with a quick, self-conscious, overwhelming thought. It's never as bad as I think: that's the point of being overwhelmed. I developed this way to differentiate some areas of thoughts in my head, as I feel I have quite a few voices to myself being bipolar,

What I want my readers to gain from my works are personal understanding and acceptance. That's what I've always wanted, I feel, as well as getting out the insane nonsense in my head. I love how when I actually get it out there it feels somewhat cohesive. I love the dopamine rush, it gives me a smile across my face.

I wanted to gain more discipline. I want to rely on writing more than smoking, drinking, mindlessly scrolling on my phone, or staring at walls or a black leak. I wouldn't say directly I hope to gain approval, but I feel like I don't want to be anything else but a writer. I tend to fantasize the days where people could just shit out stories drunk off their ass for magazines, and still have an adventurous life... not necessarily like Hemingway; more like my own personal way. I guess to say I want to be unique... I think people see it but to be honest I haven't been able to see it in myself.

This is a verbal snapshot of my personality, my thoughts, my actions, my emotions, and most importantly, it's an attempt to use a lens that's not my phone to show people the beauty of a small moment with influential, internal feelings of the scene. Not all poems chosen for this project were written in my timeline of life here, I looked upon old works and they felt presently truer than when I initially wrote them. I guess that's when looking behind my back is good for me-- it really helps me write out my future.

Blossom

I tell myself to not seem so blunt as I
break the hypotonic dissociative stare at
bath toys in lukewarm, bubbly water;
Childhood toys are gifted with
artificial happiness painted on their faces.
Should I?

I stepped outside and
while I was sad it looked like
birthday outside because I devoted
a day to childhood wonder
alongside an extra load of
errands rather than letting a mind
explore on its own.

Teaching such things is better than
filling the brain with a dull
addiction. Even if I'm just
dragging along in this life.

[There is still improvement to make].

Tonight I ended it in clapping--
I enjoyed the media worthwhile.

(Don't sit around too long, the
air is getting toxic to breathe and the
pollen is making it worse.)

I observe the colorful blossoms in frost:
I know within myself I can
bloom as well.

Closed Doors

Closed doors have frightened me
since I can remember, but
for some reason I have envied those who
could close their room door, as
I’ve rarely had the opportunity
to do so myself.

I remember when I did: I fully enjoyed
most of it, but then amongst socialization I
became irate at the idea of openness and
shared rooms; it made me afraid of
closed doors, mainly because
I wasn't willing to
open any.

Recently I’ve left doors slightly cracked open,
not as an invitation, and maybe--
I don’t know,,,
Perhaps it's for a sense
of comfort, or as if I’ve become
terrified of the creativity I am
naturally endowed with.

I now shut doors to prevent
destruction from a product I’ve
grown inside.

I am trying to learn better lessons,
because it takes a good role model
to own parenting, or to be a
better human overall.

I’m still scared of growth.

Cure

I curiously speculate about the
man across the street who feeds
stray cats while another man works on
cars with angry flashlights at
1 in the morning.

One of them lost their mother,
the other supplies the addictions.

Now I am a supplier of beer cans
for these stray cats to
straddle up in shopping carts.
We all pursue an ongoing addiction which
I can’t seem to stop enabling
beyond apprehensive actions.

I leave the supplies in plastic bags
as if to get rid of the burdens we know
are beyond my control.
I already hate myself enough, why not
fuel that dopamine I love to ignite?

I'll keep the cat food to myself, knowing
other addictions are still in need;
I'm high from the feral deserts I'm from.
I'll steal the lights from street lamps while

using a phone of my own to guide me through
fixations from a drive to home.

In the 8th grade I took home one stray cat:
A hoard of cats became the result of
empathetic motherhood.
Apologies reside in my mother's death bed.

We all still sleep the same
no matter where we lay.
I'll enjoy my mattress garnished in florals until
my habits end up burning in flames.

Airplanes and Artificial Pizza

Planes take off and land daily—
The transition always feels so long,
but it feels good experiencing a
landing rather than turbulence
against the sporadic skies.

I enjoy watching the clouds pass over the
rigid, snow cap ranges.
It's particularly mesmerizing to see the shadows
cast upon the mountain from
matter as light as a cloud.

Something of a whim holds more power than
the ruff n' tuff edges my prescribed environment
has presented to me
all my life...

The clouds will pass and the
snow will melt away to show a
raw exterior.
(Everyone glances at it. It's
destiny.)

It's still hard to get used to changes,
but, like my son, I am
learning to transition.

(Rather than waiting for a meal, you bought a machine-made pizza out in Gate A anyway.)

Seasons

When the lice gave me flowers I
found ways to make the pungent blooms
smell way worse than the early morning spring.

When flies gave my birth in shit I
didn't mind acclimating to the scorching sun.
But oh my I can't live in the trash anymore.

I made a fire to deter winter but I
turned away and wished for demise while I
smoked my mom's cigarettes after she died.

I will write down pitiful mulch to lay
so mushrooms and worms feast on my leaves.
I guess we both know who we decompose for.

Home

The early Portland morning glimmered through
blacked out eyes trying to find a way home.
The wrong trains always come at the
right time.

The sounds of amphibians playing music with
screwdrivers guide the city's mania
through a blue line.

The reflection of the MAX strives in
taking things too far and
circles of 3 show how everyone here is
connected--
everything is just a result from
everyone living their life.

I stumbled into my home and hit the
nursery's bed of flowers.
I was told I would find a way to
be paid back, but haven't I
already gotten that from living in the
city of roses basically
alone?

I rise in bed. I can't remember much:
My night was a collection of

live photos that will indefinitely
replay in my head, not in shame but
in fondness. Embarrassment still is included
in the slideshows' aftermath.

I fell and I
mumbled and I
pissed and I
sang the best my
poisoned lips could manage and I
loved life:
(The parts I can remember).

I manage to be a
mother of the morning,
but I was trembling when
making food;
I choose responsibility and fun over
mediation: How the fuck does someone
manage to do both of that?

I guess I am lucky to strive through
the replenishing consequences I always
seem to serve myself.

That night was still worth it.

Air

I think I like smoking cigarettes because
in the act I'm
just no one I'm
everywhere in my head or I'm
alleviated from a part of myself or my
life for a moment.

All I am is smoke:
I suffocate. I replicate, and I
burn with inhalation and the flick of
the match.

I am breath. I am sweet relief from a
spinning ball in the sky that just
won't stop even if we all beg 'til our
demise.

I am the atmosphere. I take in everything
and somehow still keep things
alive.

I am an environment. I am
beautiful enough to nourish, but I
enable myself to mistreatment.

"I have an actual life."

"I wish I could start acting like it."
"I love Modest Mouse and I love myself."

The longer I stay up the longer I
want to be the person I wanna be:
(You no longer want to be alive).

Maybe I should imply that to my reality--
We'll see.

East Bound

I feel growth while staring at a colorful,
budding bush in front of me.
I wonder why I am standing in this direction?
All I can think about is reproduction:
We're all a part of each other's journey to bloom.

I am usually looking back on my past:
truly the only thing which feels
real against my perception of reality.

I refuse to stare at the
Southern conifer's silhouette where I
currently reside now because my mother
always told me to sleep against the North.

The West is manipulated to be
off limits by no other than myself,
and staring up at the Northern water tower
revealed an exposure to a demise I knew
coming.

Eastern glow of houses with snapshot
windows to peak into the light of
other peoples' lives somehow alleviates me
with directions longing for a home.

I take one inhalation for self-growth
and exhale for
self-deprecation.

The Grass that Grows in Sidewalks

The street lamps get in my way and now I
don’t have a choice but to walk on the
sidewalks.
I no longer litter my sins, however
all I see along the streets is trash.

I revive my drive to walk as
much as possible although it
lacks the magic like it used to.

I am listening to music again
and I see augmentations
through my life more than ever, but it
doesn’t feel like deja vu anymore.

Maybe I don't care anymore.
Maybe it was influential. Maybe I was
inspired from watching it in real
life before.

I begin to stab at the grass in the cracks of
the sidewalks, trying to prevent growth.
Stepping over litter as if I am walking around
in my own apartment.

Realism

I am a street lamp
I love to shine down on people
while walking through their darkest days,
I brighten the walks along the way.
Sometimes I can be blinding,
but few know this is me shining.

I am a water tower
I hold in the tears just so
other people can stay hydrated,
If someone taps me right
I will burst and
always end up feeling worse.

I am a city's rainy day which
makes sure everyone else is aware of
the reasons why I am crying
Not merely saying I want to die, but
somehow a sunshine makes it beautiful--
I still have a life I wanna fulfill.

I am an outcast day in the fields
and in the mountains and
in the stream; I feel so verdant;
It's never been this serene.

The route has to end soon.
I got to go back to reality again.

I am pressing on the breaks amongst
the freeway of people who are trying to
get by: Not one of us knows how to drive.
We get merely by; let's just
keep ourselves and our cars alive.

Just please let me get in my own lane.

Traveling

I constantly go through change.
Being sedentary makes the ground crumble
beneath while my feet still feel alive.
Traveling builds a hopeful,
solitary foundation to build upon--
Staying in one places makes my
posture sore.

It's as if I'm going through all these
live events as though I am forced to
sit emotionlessly behind the driver's wheel--
seeing places and people and cars that have a
life, but
mine feels too personal to decipher on what can
be
better or worse-- Emotions take too much into
play.

Visual remembrance is traumatic as well as
beautiful--
Most of it was lived in darkness, but memory
strives to know the whole story through
art, writing, and relations' most abled thoughts.

I somehow captured that perfectly; a

3" by 3" canvas with fine wine detail and ghastly
vignette border
with sappy sucker emotions getting in the way
of
what the thought was saturated in origin.

Being ripped away from what seemed like
a home hurts more than birth.
I still remember that 3AM morning where I
prolonged
an album's sickness before I could swallow
dramamine:
I nursed a baby in the parking lot until 5AM.
I had to yank him off the tit in order to
no longer be car sick.

I saw numbers on a hill which reminded me
of how I'm getting older.
I wonder how many birthdays I have
left to gain strength?
How much longer until I feel ground
strong enough to settle on?

We drove on, high from induced mania through
a
Christmas's Valley into a vomit-green forest full
of paralysis demons to
what I was forced to call home.
It was nice when we were in park.

The Hands That Gives a Baby Fruit

I woke up to the desperate cry of babies, but
couldn't distinct attention
from neglect. Not like much of us ever had an
open choice to begin with;
I reach with my hands out to the life I've created.

I walked to the door to expose myself to life and
saw a pattern of
orange ashes splattered like paint on my
evening's route.
Some of it got inside, though I do not know how.

I then threw the clementine's peels out with my
dominant hand
while reaching out weakly with the right
initiative to
feed the child in front of me.

Today everyone is displaying their left hand
eccentrically,
or lack thereof.
As if it were something I should pay more
attention to.

As if I don't already feel this world is only mine,
and I have

something to do about all of this.

The weather here won’t stop being moody and it's hard to get along with the bare space between unwanted fingertips.

Friendship

I’ve seen my friends grow more
into real people the
farther I’m away from them as if I’m writing a
terrible story in a weird form of
self-consciousness.

These people breathe like me and
make decisions good and bad and oh I'm
starting to think I understand life beyond
these paranoid lenses I sport daily.

My friends are not my addictions:
They have shown me that there's
better ways out, but I guess I love
seeing them happier than me.

Isn’t that what I always had to strive for?
Making sure everything is ok before
I am?
I was a child, then a friend, then a mother... I've
only learned to think for others.

3:32 AM

Drawing lines in death, oh how it feels good
to have something against my wrist-- I'm
sensitive to the real thing now, which is
something I've rarely felt before.

I've concocted abuse within my mind,
thinking everything is against me, yet
somehow I am totally fine.

Artwork bleeds through my mind but
my blood is poisoned so why
cry over spilt milk when I can
write my truer heart's content for the night?

I wonder when will my credit be paid off?

I swallow liquid more than food and I
neglect my moods through suppression by
work at home and a mile away but
now it's 3AM and this love poem is
going nowhere.

Someday he will leave home, you know.

Yellow Flowers

Stand before me while I stare
impatiently upon flowers as if their
bloom will affect the life I'm trying to
get by;
I think they're getting uncomfortable.

It's almost as if they are waiting for
me to take a turn, but we will be
pointing guns at each other if it
reaches to that point.

A soft, imaginative hand touches
my shoulder and says
look again tomorrow.

I'll wake up with a playful incentive
to take on the day.

When I Think of Death,

pains in my body don't ache as much
as the ones in my spoiled mind.
(I'll try not to get too behind.)

The leaves of the trees go missing, but
grass is verdant no matter what
(at least for here, at least for now).

The flowers bloom though you
know beauty doesn’t last forever.
(You still live vicariously through vegetation.)

The red rim around the moon is visible
but those lights can be changed, right?
(You either die or the scab heals.)

I cover the pavement with wishful ash although
I still throw the cigarette butts away.
(That'll be you someday soon.)

Leaves

Maybe I'm just a cunt--
A big ol' cunt who suppresses
thoughts like these and engage in
manic activities which leads me to
hiding things among the trash that align
the streets of my city's lines.

Sometimes I walk through life with annoyance:
Anger that I know there could be better, but
other times I wander alongside wonder thinking
I
can truly make this world a livable experience
without
noticing themes around my home's boundaries.

I know the symbolisms' of songs we enjoy
resonate between us, in polar interpretations,
and perhaps I do know why my
Mom is no longer with us.
I've never been able to be myself until now
though.

[But myself is shit.]

Elevation

Mountains that are mighty somehow
seem different in my direct vision every time I
study them in the distant journey along the
expressway.

It’s hard to slow down, considering external
forces--
oh how they are forcing me to keep up the pace.

Sometimes I’ll stare in awe, wondering how
something always seems to be changing.
It's the one thing I strive to see and
even more so conquer.

I didn’t have visions like these before, and I
admit:
mountains are harder to see beyond when I’m
used to striding on the flat farmland.

The visionary can wander while insights
stay the same. I’m closer than
ever before to what I want to become.

It’s easy to lose sight when I’m merely
cruising within a mountain range's valley,

but sometimes it’s just nice to vibe by yourself
while
having the comfort of a strange vehicle besides
you
for a minute.
(You both end up in the same lane for a bit.)

Strains

"Yes, I really know what I have to do."
"But I actually have to do them."
(But you———————————————— but
you actually............ have to......... do them).

The Rain

I had to stop staring at
blinding light because moments before
I realized I found out my life is
going towards a dark water tower.
(There is a faint light shining
right behind it.)

It claims everything I'm hiding
underneath. It is near my home,
as well my route to the MAX where I
celebrate the infancy of life in the city,
as well as my work or mail which occasionally
gets stolen from me financially.

The first night here I saw a tent camp
caught on fire before I looked upon
that water tower. I will later grow
comfort and wonder on how my
Mom would die.

I wasn't truly wrong.

Occasionally I've been drawn to the
circular motions of darkness;
Liquids behold consumption
because I solely know

that's all I need to survive-- it's
all I served for purpose in life.

Rain goes on 3 days in a row here;
"Amanda? Please fill up my water bottle."

I hate looking back at the light,
yet I'm always intrigued while I
avoid the shining path ahead.
The unknown standards of beauty
seem to be out of grasp for me.

Free Shoes

I stomp along dusty, rocky trails
with tears perpetuated by a
thin, glowing block in the distance--
it seems irredeemable:
I shall strive for it anyway.

I know things are neutral, but
my mood swings carry my
polar opposite limbs
to a top of a cliff, where I
desired a sunset, but only saw
blue clouds and translucent
mountains.

I scrape my knees whether my
predictions of the sky are true or
false. I know when I need to quit the act;
The thrill to the top is so much fun
and I need to have an audience.

I smiled amidst the wind
standing towards the edge,
still carrying sunshine along the
ups and downs of our lives which I can
only control. Still, I
have a hard time going through it

with my true mind regressing
in the distance.

I'm coming down again--
I admit I overreacted
(I have more dirty laundry to do).
I keep silent the rest of the evening,
and in favor the valley was kissed
with a (light) comfort of rain.

(You were looking forward to this anyway.)

www.ingramcontent.com/pod-product-compliance
Lightning Source LLC
Chambersburg PA
CBHW062109140826
49812CB00058B/977